I0200499

This Means War

~ Workbook ~

By:
Chakita S. Hargrove
Pastor Calvin E. Callins, Sr.
Dr. Tandria M. Callins

Heart Ink Press LLC

Since 2009

Tallahassee • Plant City

Copyright © 2015 by Chakita S. Hargrove, Calvin E. Callins, Sr. and Tandria M. Callins

All rights reserved. This book is protected under the copyright laws of the United States of America. This book may not be copied or reprinted for commercial gain or profit. No portion of this book may be reproduced, stored in a retrieval system, or transmitted in any form or by any means—electronic, mechanical, photocopy, recording, scanning, or other—without the prior written permission of the author. Brief quotations in critical reviews or articles are not permitted without the consent of the author. Permissions will be granted upon request.

ISBN 978-0-9835854-8-0

Heart.Ink Press
www.heartinkpress.com
Tuned to the beat of your heart
Manifesting dreams and visions

Printed in the United States of America

Table of Contents

Preface

The time has come for us to get bold, stand up, put on our armor and declare that it is war time. For far too long people have allowed themselves to live in bondage longer than what God had ever intended for them to be. Passiveness has overtaken a person's will to get up and fight, to declare war against the "enemy", and claim victory.

The word enemy was placed in quotation marks because you must first define and acknowledge who and what your enemy is. The enemy in your case may be a relationship, fear, yourself, finances, Satan, and et cetera. Throughout this workbook you will be tasked with doing a self-evaluation, putting the spotlight on yourself, standing underneath a magnifying glass, having an inner exploration of what is causing you to be in bondage and in a state of worry and flight.

You must also understand that war doesn't involve you always balling up your fists, grabbing a carnal weapon (i.e. gun or sword), and screaming obscenities to be heard to win.

Prayer and worship can be your form of weapon during war.

Grab yourself something to write with and let's get ready to explore. Recognizing who and what the enemy is, is the first step in learning how to fight and deal with the enemy so that you may be victorious and liberated.

Now, before you move on we need to say one thing, "Don't allow fear to cause you to not call out your bondage (enemy)."

This Means War!

- **Chakita S. Hargrove, Pastor Calvin E. Callins, Sr., and Dr. Tandria M. Callins**

Jehoshaphat: Don't Worry, Just Worship

Scripture: 1 Kings 22:1-50; 2 Kings 3;

2 Chronicles 17:1 - 21:3

King Jehoshaphat reigned for 25-years and during his reign he remained devoted to the Lord. He not once converted to the religious practices of the neighboring nation, Israel, nor that of the many kings of Judah. Much of Jehoshaphat's story serves as a record of his religious reforms. Jehoshaphat's most memorable moment is when he and his nation were surrounded by an alliance of three vast armies that were ready to attack.

King Jehoshaphat recognized that he was in a helpless position and so he hosted a nationwide day of prayer. The Lord answered the prayers and told Jehoshaphat that he would defeat his enemies without fighting. Jehoshaphat trusted in the Lord with no doubt that he dispatched an army; an army not of soldiers, but that of singers who sung praises to God. When the dispatched army came upon the invaders, they discovered that the invaders were completely destroyed by internal fighting.

King Jehoshaphat facing three armies was indeed his greatest crisis, for it was a situation that could have exterminated him and his nation. Think about it, three nations joined together with one purpose in mind, and that was to invade, destroy, and overtake. Scouting by Jehoshaphat's men revealed that the three nation army was nearby and that Judah was far overpowered.

Jehoshaphat didn't runaway at the report that he received. He didn't shout out, "Every man for himself!" He stood as the King and declared that everyone prays. The entire population assembled together at Jerusalem and they in unity fasted and prayed. King Jehoshaphat's prayer expressed God's might, His history and promise of aid to His people. Jehoshaphat acknowledged their present helplessness and ended his prayer by saying, "We do not know what to do, but our eyes are upon you" (2 Chronicles 20:12).

As the people waited, the Lord spoke through prophet Jahaziel, instructing the army to fearlessly march against the invaders, take up their battle positions, and watch the Lord fight the battle for them. The army would not have to fight at all. King Jehoshaphat and the people were relieved and worshipped the Lord.

Early the next morning, King Jehoshaphat assembled his army. Since God had told him that they wouldn't have to fight, the army was then not led by the bravest soldiers, but by the choir. The army marched to meet their enemy while singing praises to God. As the three nation army heard the army of Judah approaching, singing, they became confused. The armies began to bicker with one another and eventually killed one another. By the time King Jehoshaphat's army reached the battlefield, there was no sign of a survivor.

Jehoshaphat's army was then organized into a work force to carry away everything valuable. It took them three days to collect all the goods. Intense celebration took place and news spread of Judah's victory to the nearby kingdoms that no one waged war against Judah for the rest of King Jehoshaphat's reign.

Self-Exploration

How would you handle a situation like the one Jehoshaphat encountered?

_____

_____

_____

Would you have formed an alliance with the sinning nations who worshipped idol gods just to save yourself, or would you remain faithful and adhere to the word of God concerning what it is that you are to do?

_____

_____

Do you currently find yourself surrounded by three armies? If so, what are they?

1. _____

_____

2. _____

_____

3. _____

_____

What can you do to defeat those armies?

_____

_____

_____

_____

King Jehoshaphat didn't have to encounter the three nation army alone. Do you have an individual or individuals who are willing to go into battle with you? _____ If so, who?

_____

_____

A Word of Thought

Sometimes being in a war puts us in a place of worry instead of worship. If you find yourself constantly worrying about every battle and every attack, fearful to fight and claim victory, you need to find the strength to go into worship. Seek the face of God and ask for His instructions. As King Jehoshaphat closed out his prayer, to make it personal, "I don't know what to do, but my eyes are upon you." Wait for the answer, God's instruction(s), and adhere to what He says.

A Parable: Left Wounded

Scripture: Luke 10:25-33

A situation occurred where an expert in religious law had an encounter with Jesus. He tested Jesus by asking Him how he could inherit eternal life. Jesus' reply to the man consisted of two questions, "What does the law of Moses say?" and "How do you read it?" The expert gave his response and Jesus agreed, but the man asked Jesus yet another question, "who is my neighbor?" Thus begins a parable that Jesus shares with the man.

For this chapter, we are going to look at just verse 30, "Jesus replied with a story: 'A Jewish man was traveling from Jerusalem down to Jericho, and he was attacked by bandits. They stripped him of his clothes, beat him up, and left him half dead beside the road.'"

Experiences in life might have left you exposed and vulnerable to public scrutiny and shame. Old scars and current open wounds are visible for the world to see. You have been attacked so many times that you find yourself laying in your own blood and bed of sorrow. You feel as though life is leaving you and your desire to maintain the little life that you believe you have left is slowly depleting because you are too weak to fight for your own life, too busy waiting for someone else to come to your rescue, resting in pity to be recognized, and yet people continue to pass you by. No one is acknowledging your wounds.

The parable later shares that a priest crossed the road as to not walk up closely pass the man who was left for dead, and a temple assistant walked over and saw him laying there and then walked across the street. Expecting help from a certain type of people may have you lying beside the road half dead for a long time. Even though a Samaritan eventually came along, you shouldn't sulk in your wounds and wait for man to help you. You need to find that inner will to live and survive every attack that comes your way. You need to find your voice and determination to live and not die; to not allow the enemy to destroy your desire to live.

You have to fight to keep that which you know God has given you. This means war! You have been in a place of being beat up, wounded, and defeated for far too long. It is time to open up your mouth and shout "no more!" Defeat is no longer an answer and your wounds should no longer put you in a place of embarrassment and depression. The wounds will heal and the scars are just a sign of where you have been, not where you are going.

Tell yourself, "I am about to fight back." Again, passiveness is not the answer. Even with your wounds you begin to speak victory and not defeat. You begin to declare that change is coming and that you will no longer be a target for slaughter. Understand that as a child of God, your words have power and that which you speak is spirit and life (John 6:63).

Don't get upset when the people you expect to come to your rescue, to help you, are nowhere to be found. Become your own cheerleader and self-motivator. Speak life into yourself and have the self-confidence that you are well able to defeat the enemy with the help of the Lord. Reliance on others can cripple you and cause you to lose faith in your own ability and power.

Self-Exploration

What kind of wounds do you currently have that need to be healed?

_____

_____

_____

_____

How do you currently handle or manage the wounds that you have?

_____

_____

How long do you typically sulk in your sorrow and throw yourself a pity-party? _____

Who do you typically expect to help you no matter what your problem is?

_____

_____

Has the person(s) you listed ever failed to come to your rescue/aid? _____ **If the answer is "yes", how did that make you feel?**

_____

_____

_____

A Word of Thought

It is written in Isaiah 41:13 that the Lord will hold you by your right hand and that you shouldn't be afraid because He will help you. If you stop running to man for help and actually consider God as your first choice for help, then things can possibly be better for you. Laying half dead, wounded and alone doesn't have to be your predicament if you rely on the right person to help you fight for your life and heal your wounds.

Just Say No: Stop Being an Enabler

Scripture: 2 Thessalonians 3:10-15

The reasons why an individual may feel used, manipulated, and exploited are reasons that take the blame away from the individual who feels used, manipulated, and exploited. Individuals are quick to blame the abuser while never seeing that he or she is serving as the enabler of the abuse. The truth is that you allow people to use you, manipulate you, and exploit you; for whatever reason it is hard for you to say "no."

To enable is to make able. To give power, means, competence, or ability to. To authorize. To make possible or easy. To make ready or to equip. You give people the tools to use, manipulate, and exploit you by your not having the ability to say "no."

If you do not get to the point of truly being tired of being used, manipulated, and exploited, you will continue to say "yes." You will continue to come to the rescue, you will continue to allow your services to yield no reward to you, and you will continue to feel underappreciated. Believe it or not, you can control how you allow people to treat you. You have control over what you are willing to do.

Being Used

You allow people to use you because you believe that the task is simple, you do not want to disappoint those who will benefit from the task being completed, you respect the position and the authority of the individual, or you want to belong and you like to be relied upon.

Being Manipulated

People are able to manipulate your feelings because they know how to manage and skillfully influence you, especially in an unfair manner. Once a person knows your weaknesses (your inability to say "no"), he or she becomes equipped and thus adapts or changes to attract your weakness to suit his or her own purpose or advantage.

Being Exploited

Those who know your character (i.e. kindness, helpfulness, etc.) will utilize that knowledge to profit themselves. Your inability to say "no" can attract selfish people who want to advance or be promoted through exploitation (exploiting you).

You can stop being an enabler by creating healthy boundaries. You must gain sanity in your life by stopping your own negative behaviors (the behaviors of an enabler). Before you can stop being an enabler, you must first admit that you are in fact an enabler.

Those who are enablers often need an accountability partner because when it comes to matters involving both the heart and the mind, it is a decision that must be made with a great deal of prayer and discussion. You must be convinced of the need to stop repeating your negative, enabling behaviors. You have to be ready, willing, and able to give the process of change your total commitment.

The most painful step in any healing process is often the first. You must face the ugly truth that you are in a destructive relationship and that you are the one who has allowed it to continue. As long as you minimize the truth about your problem, you cannot become strong enough to challenge or change anything.

You should not ignore your own personal issues because they just may be why you are an enabler. You can become an enabler as a result of guilt over perceived failures (the feeling that you must somehow compensate for your past failures as a person, parent, and or friend). You can become an enabler to fulfill the need to be appreciated by the individual(s) you enable. You can become an enabler in order to be an influence. You can become an enabler in order to compensate for the love and the physical needs you were deprived as a youth. You can also become an enabler as a result of the lack of trust in God for the outcome; for example, if you cut off the flow of money or any other form of enablement.

There is a difference between being supportive or helpful and enabling. It is okay to provide financial support as long as it is not enabling a dangerous lifestyle (i.e. addiction). Constantly cleaning up a person's mess (i.e. bailing out of jail, covering for when a person misses work or school) is the action of an enabler. You're always coming through takes away the responsibility that the individual must have for his or her own actions and life. The fear of confronting the behavior of a loved one and covering their responsibilities can mean that you are an enabler.

Be careful of the over use of "this too shall pass" and "God will take care of this." Everyone must be proactive about his or her life.

If you are not quite sure if you are an enabler or not, I only have one tip for you and that is to not ignore the funny feeling. There is typically an "off" feeling one gets when he or she believes that he or she is being used, manipulated, and exploited. Constantly ignoring that feeling makes you an enabler. Do not allow people to pimp you.

For years I have been an enabler. I have given people the right to use, manipulate, and exploit me. It hurt me to say "no" to certain people and those people knew it. It took years of disappointment and hurt to get to a breaking point and to learn the power of saying "no."

Once I took the blame for how I was being treated, I took back control of my life. I learned how to consider the outcome of saying "no." I no longer wanted to continue the cycle of under-appreciation and slavery to the will and wants of others. I wanted to experience the freedom of knowing that I have a choice and that it is my choice to make.

I stopped people from making me feel guilty for saying "no." I took back my choice and remembered my goals, ambitions, and dreams. My constant "yes" was pushing my purpose and goals to the back of my mind. Everyone and their goals, ambitions, and dreams came before my own.

I now know how to balance my use of the words "no" and "yes", and I have stopped the cycle of being an enabler. Do not get so far in your life constantly helping others until one day you wish that you would have taken time for yourself. Allow your works to benefit you and not always someone else. Like I told one of my best friends years ago, "I will help you when you start helping yourself."

Self-Exploration

Why have you allowed people to use you?

_____

_____

_____

_____

What can you do to stop the cycle of being used?

_____

_____

_____

_____

How have people been able to manipulate you?

_____

_____

_____

_____

When were you exploited and how did it make you feel?

_____

_____

_____

_____

How do you see yourself?

_____

_____

_____

_____

A Word of Thought

Learn to say "no" while encouraging your brother and/or sister to put in work to help themselves. Your inability to say "no" cripples the individual and leaves you in a place of bondage, stress, and lack. You begin to give

grudgingly and not out of the sincerity of your heart. Stop being an enabler. It won't be easy at first, but just say "no".

The Sower: Choking on Immaturity

Scripture: Luke 8:14

This chapter is not written to say that you are childish, but to say that misplaced priorities can showcase your level of maturity. Immaturity in the time of war is deadly, not just for yourself but for those who are connected to you (i.e. those who reside in your home). Luke 8:14 states that, "The seed that fell among thorns stands for those who hear, but as they go on their way they are choked by life's worries, riches and pleasures, and they do not mature."

Where are you sowing? More importantly, who are you sowing into? Your seeds are valuable and to nonchalantly give seed where the soil isn't fertile is pointless and a waste. You may have heard a word to sow, but you moved so quickly that you didn't ask God: Where to sow? Who to sow into? When to sow? How much to sow? So what you have done is sown a seed that now has you choking on life's worries, riches and pleasures. Simply put, as the word says, your seed doesn't mature.

Proverbs 27:20 puts it like this, "Hell and destruction are never full; so the eyes of man are never satisfied." The war that you might be experiencing is caused by your immaturity in discernment and financial self-control. It's time to grow up, know who you serve, and know the power that you have.

Speak against leeches; people who are in your life to manipulate you and suck you dry from everything you have earned and have been blessed with by God. It's wartime against your finances. God wants His children to be prosperous.

> **Deuteronomy 5:33**, "Stay on the path that the Lord your God has commanded you to follow. Then you will live long and prosperous lives in the land you are about to enter and occupy."

> **Matthew 6:33**, "Seek the Kingdom of God above all else, and live righteously,

and he will give you everything you need."

It is time to war against whatever has your finances not meeting your needs. We aren't saying to simply pray against some principality that is consuming your finances, but we are also saying to practice self-control and live within your means. If it hasn't been stated before, it is being stated now...some wars you cause yourself.

Self-Exploration

How often have you found yourself in a financial bind? _____

What or who is the cause of the financial hardship? _____

_____

_____

When do you notice that you vainly spend or make vain purchases? _____

_____

_____

Who are your leeches?

1. _____

_____

2. _____

_____

3. _____

_____

Put a plan in place to budget your finances and practice saying "no" to your leeches.

A Word of Thought

Take back control of your finances by giving God what's due Him, saying no to the leeches, and creating a budget. Immaturely giving, planting seeds in thorns and on unfertile ground produces nothing that's mature enough to yield fruit. Use discernment in seed planting. Take back control of your finances so that you can end your season of choking on life's worries, riches and pleasures.

Speak It: Changing the Atmosphere of Your Life

Scripture: Exodus 9:29 and Proverbs 16:24

Words can bless a person or they can curse a person. Words will heal or make you sick. How you speak about yourself and others has a direct bearing on what the mind creates. Words that ridicule, torment, harass and tear down a person will never bring life. Thoughts that are always fearful and bitter will never remove fear and worry. The Lord says our thoughts are not His (READ Isaiah 55:8-9), but they can be His if we will change our way of thinking and speaking. The wars that you have is possibly because you have spoken it into existence (READ Romans 4:17). How you change your atmosphere has much to do with what you speak, think, and do.

Phrases like the following will lift the heart and mind and restore life: "My words work for me. I fill them with a power that cannot be resisted. I fill my words with faith and love. My words bless. My words heal. My words lead my loved ones into victory. My words charge the atmosphere of my home with faith and love. I am a winner, I am a champion, I am the healed of the Lord, I walk in righteousness in Jesus Christ, and I am a new creation. The old inner person is gone and the new person lives in Christ Jesus."

What you say and think makes a difference in your life. Your words are the keys to abundant life. Unlock the door to your life of abundance by keeping a watch on what you say, think, and do. In any situation you have to be able to "Power Speak" in order to change the atmosphere of your situation. You won't be able to effectively do this if your heart is not right. READ Luke 6:45, Matthew 15:18, and Deuteronomy 30:14

Hosea 14:2 (NIV) reads, "Take words with you and return to the LORD. Say to him: 'Forgive all our sins and receive us graciously, that we may offer the fruit of our lips.'" To "Power Speak" yourself into heavenly places and/or to change your atmosphere, you have to bring words to Christ that is pure and sincere. Let nothing hinder you from getting to Christ;

your atmosphere must change. The war must end.

Here are some "Power Speak" phrases:

1. When someone tries to bring up your past, or you feel unworthy or unqualified because of your past.

   a. I have repented of my sins and surrendered my life to my Lord Jesus Christ (I John 1:9)

   b. I am born again (John 3:3, I Peter 1:22-23, I John 1:7)

   c. I am a new creature (II Corinthians 5:17)

2. When you feel like you don't belong or you are in the wrong place.

   a. I am a child of God (I John 5:1)

b. **My steps are ordered by the Lord (Psalms 37:23)**

3. **When you need to feel security.**

   a. **The angel of the Lord encamps about me to protect me (Psalms 34:7)**

4. **When you are having an identity crisis and are questioning your ability.**

   a. **I am a king and a priest in Christ Jesus (Revelation 1:6)**

   b. **All things work together for my good (Romans 8:28)**

   c. **I am more than a conqueror through Christ who loves me (Romans 8:37)**

5. When thoughts of failure are lurking about.

    a. **God always causeth me to triumph in Christ (II Corinthians 2:14)**

    b. **Many are the afflictions of the righteous: but the Lord delivereth him out of them all (Psalms 34:19)**

6. When sickness hits you.

    a. **By the stripes of Jesus I am healed (I Peter 2:24)**

7. When you feel week.

    a. **I have power with God (John 14:13-14)**

8. When you start experiencing issues with people and a strong dislike begins to stir up in your spirit.

a. I love everybody (Matthew 5:44)

9. When you have experienced a rough day.

    a. Today is the best day of my life (Romans 8:28, Proverbs 4:18)

    b. Tomorrow will be better (Romans 8:28, Proverbs 4:18)

10. When you can't find the words to say.

    a. Hallelujah!

    b. Thank you Jesus!

Self-Exploration

On a typical day, what type of atmosphere do your words create? _____

_____

_____

On a typical day, what type of atmosphere does your thoughts and behaviors create? ____

_____

_____

When you are going through or are experiencing a tough situation, what do you usually say or do? _____

_____

_____

_____

A Word of Thought

Your words have power, so be careful how you use them. It is stated in James 1:26 that "If you claim to be religious but don't control your tongue, you are fooling yourself, and your religion is worthless." Stop being a constant negative speaker and begin to change your atmosphere with your words. Your words can cause wars and it can also bring an end to them.

Get Up: Take Your Territory

Scripture: Numbers 33:52-53

Traveling down a road and passing a piece of property that used to be yours can be heartbreaking and depressing. Your mind begins to travel back in time and you begin to reminisce on what was and you begin to think on what could be or what could have been. You find yourself getting upset that you have allowed your property to go and you begin to ask yourself, "How could I have let this happen?" As you continue to travel down the road you start blaming others for not helping you keep what you have lost. It's not until you go down your list of contacts, blaming everyone, that you finally realize that YOU lost your territory (property); not your family, friends, and anyone else you choose to blame.

It is stated in Numbers 33:52-53 that, "you must drive out all the people living there. You must destroy all their carved and molten images and demolish all their pagan shrines. Take possession of the land and settle in it, because I have given it to you to occupy."

Territory that is intended to be yours might be occupied by someone else, but if God says that it is yours then it is yours. Claiming your territory may require you to put some work in; diligent effort. Hopefully you did not believe that every promise of God to you will come quickly and with ease.

Here are some steps to take back your territory (this list is not exhaustive):

1st – <u>Start out with praise.</u> The Israelites asked the Lord, "Who will be the first to go into battle?" The Lord said, "Judah is to go; I have given the land into their hands." Judah means: to "Praise." You are to send praise forth first and then the land will be given into your hands. (Judges 1:1-2)

2nd – <u>You will need to repent and ask the Lord for His forgiveness for your sins.</u> Leviticus 26:40 – If they will confess their sins and the sins of their fathers- their treachery against me and their hostility toward me, which made me hostile toward them so that I sent them into the land of their enemies-THEN- when their uncircumcised hearts are humbled and they pay for their sin, I will remember my covenant with them and I will remember the land.

3rd – <u>Pray to break spiritual cords, ties, and chains</u> (Spiritual Warfare)

Judges 6:25 – (1) Tear down your fathers altar to Baal. (2) Then build a proper kind of altar to the Lord your God.

4th – <u>Shout a victory cry to the Lord and blow the Shofar at the four corners of the city at the same time.</u> 1 Chronicles 15:28 – Israel came before the Lord with shouts, with the sounding of rams horns and trumpets.

5th – <u>Settle and possess the land so that you are not scattered.</u> Numbers 33:51-53 – When you cross over into your land, drive out all your enemies of the land before you. Destroy their idols and demolish all their high places. Take possession of the land and settle in it, for I have given you the land to possess.

6th – <u>Anoint and devote your territory to the Lord.</u> Joshua 6:20-21 – When the trumpets sounded, the people shouted, and at the sound of the trumpet, when the people gave a loud shout, the wall collapsed; so every man charged straight in, and they took the city. They devoted (anointed) the city to the Lord.

Self-Exploration

Have you lost something that you wish you could have back? _____ What is it?

_____

_____

Was there a moment in your life when you quit trying? _____ If yes, why? _____

_____

_____

Do you realize that every promise is not placed in your lap? _____

Do you know the steps to obtain your territory or promise? _____ If yes, what are the steps? _____

_____

_____

If no, then what are you going to do to get the answer? _____

_____

_____

How hard are you willing to work to obtain your territory or promise? _____

_____

_____

_____

_____

Are you willing to work even harder to keep your territory or promise? _____

A Word of Thought

2 Samuel 22:31 lets us know that "God's way is perfect. All the LORD's promises prove true. He is a shield for all who look to him for protection." Even if you may have lost your territory and you know that God has promised

the territory to you, just remember that God's way is perfect and His word will manifest. If you are required to go into the enemies' camp to take back that which is yours, the scripture continues to say that "He is a shield for all who look to him for protection."

Know Your Identity: Take Back Your Life

Scripture: James 1:23-24

James 1:23-14 puts it like this, "Anyone who listens to the word but does not do what it says is like someone who looks at his face in a mirror and, after looking at himself, goes away and immediately forgets what he looks like."

Whose dreams are you living? Whose ambitions are you fulfilling? If they are not your own then you may need to step back and evaluate what is going on in your life. Living someone else's life as your own is labeled as a crime; you are committing identity fraud or identity theft. You are not being obedient to the word that God has given you concerning your life. Ephesians 2:10 states that "For we are his workmanship, created in Christ Jesus unto good works, which God hath before ordained that we should walk in them."

What good works were you created to walk in? What is it that you desire for your life? How do you envision your life going? Have you always wanted your life to consist of the burden of living someone else's life for them? If not, then it is time for you to take back your life!

There has to come a point in time when you are ready to live for you. This change in your life may make you feel guilty of solely focusing on you, and people may say that you are selfish. But just as people take vacations from work and church, you need to take a break from living for other people.

It is time for you to step to the forefront of your own life. Have you accomplished your own desires and dreams? Have you paused your purpose in life to make sure that someone fulfills his or her purpose? You must bring balance to your life, and you must stop abusing your own self while allowing others to do the same.

Abuse is defined as regularly or repeatedly treating a person (or animal) with cruelty or violence; to misuse. Abuse can come in the form of coercive behaviors that are used to maintain power and control. There are several kinds of abuse that can be divided into six categories: physical (hitting, shoving); emotional (guilt trips, mind games); verbal (threats, yelling); sexual (unwanted touch of any kind); financial (controlling money flow); and social (isolation, spreading rumors). It is true that many people who are being abused do not see themselves as victims and that is partially because they cannot admit that they are being abused.

Take a moment and consider if you have been abused.

Physically

_____

_____

Emotionally

_____

_____

Verbally

_____

_____

Sexually

_____

_____

Financially

_____

_____

Socially

_____

_____

How have you let the abuse affect your life?

_____

_____

_____

_____

Abuse can be paralyzing and can control your life if you allow it to. From experience, I have learned that I control how things will affect me. I was once a prisoner of affirmation. I felt like I needed ratification and confirmation from people. It took years for me to break free from that desire. Some people may say that my new found freedom comes off sometimes as a bad thing because now I can care less what a person says or thinks concerning me and that is because I have accepted who I am and how I function. I have learned that I had to stop seeking what I couldn't get from people.

You should not live your life for others, nor should you let people live your life for you. What you do should be your choice. You should not allow people to dictate what you do with all your time, who your friends are, where you work, what degree you should get in college, how you wear your hair, how you dress, what you say and how you say it, where you live, what church you go to, what ministry or auxiliary you should be a part of, how you spend your money, and so forth.

Once you have taken back your life, do not easily give it up again. If you have to, fight for your life. You may just have to let go of some people (i.e. family, friends, church people, etc.) to maintain control of your life. Have you ever had a friend who always wanted things to go his or her way? That person is the controller, often hidden behind the title leader.

Stop being passive and weak about your life. Passive is defined as not reacting visible to something that might be expected to produce manifestations of an emotion or feeling, not participating readily or actively (inactive). You must be an active participant in your life. Stop holding everything (i.e. emotions, words, and your true choice) in. React! As it has been stated multiple times already, take back your life. It's war time!

Self-Exploration
What is it that you want out of life? Take a moment and write what you want down.

_____

_____

_____

_____

_____

_____

_____

_____

_____

_____

A Word of Thought

What you have written down should serve as a visual reminder of what it is that you want out of life. What you want may change, and that is okay. Just make sure that it is your choice; that you are not being negatively influenced or manipulated to change what you want in life. Galatians 5:1 says, "Stand fast therefore in the liberty wherewith Christ hath made us free,

and be not entangled again with the yoke of
bondage."

Family Stuff: Breaking the Inherited

Scripture: Ezekiel 18:19-32

There are instances when children begin to reap the chastisement intended for their parents because of the sins that their parents have committed and have never sought forgiveness for. However, an opportunity presents itself where the child will no longer be responsible for the sin of the parent, and the parent be not responsible for the sin of the child. The problem becomes that the child does not know another way of living besides that which he or she has been taught and has observed from his or her parents and so it seems that the child is reaping the chastisement of his or her parents when in actuality the child is being chastised for his or her own actions.

The time has come to break the mental and emotional chains that keep you bound to the lifestyle you were raised in. The time has come for you to ask God for a renewed mind and a new way of living in Him. The time has come for you step out of the shadows of what was and stop blaming your parents for the way that you are. The time has come for you to take responsibility for your own actions and break loose from that family stuff that has been having you in bondage. It's time to break the inherited!

Ezekiel 18:19-32 is provided in its entirety so that you can consistently read it until you either feel the breaking of the inherited or to simply remind you that you are reaping the punishment of your own choices and actions.

"'What?' you ask. 'Doesn't the child pay for the parent's sins?' No! For if the child does what is just and right and keeps my decrees, that child will surely live. The person who sins is the one who will die. The child will not be punished for the parent's sins, and the parent will not be punished for the child's sins. Righteous people will be rewarded for their own righteous behavior, and wicked people will be punished for their own wickedness. But if wicked people turn away from all their sins and begin to obey my decrees and do what is just and right, they will surely live and not die. All their past sins will be forgotten, and they will live because of the righteous things they have done.

"Do you think that I like to see wicked people die? says the Sovereign LORD. Of course not! I want them to turn from their wicked ways and live. However, if righteous people turn from their righteous behavior and start doing sinful things and act like other sinners, should they be allowed to live? No, of course not! All their righteous acts will be forgotten, and they will die for their sins.

"Yet you say, 'The Lord isn't doing what's right!' Listen to me, O people of Israel. Am I the one not doing what's right, or is it you? When righteous people turn from their righteous behavior and start doing sinful things, they will die for it. Yes, they will die because of their sinful deeds. And if wicked people turn from their wickedness, obey the law, and do what is just and right, they will save their lives. They will live because they thought it over and decided to turn from their sins. Such people will not die. And yet the people of Israel keep saying, 'The Lord isn't doing what's right!' O people of Israel, it is you who are not doing what's right, not I.

"Therefore, I will judge each of you, O people of Israel, according to your actions, says the Sovereign LORD. Repent, and turn from your sins. Don't let them destroy you! Put all your rebellion behind you, and find yourselves a new heart and a new spirit. For why should you die, O people of Israel? I don't want you to die, says the Sovereign LORD. Turn back and live!

Self-Exploration

What hardships have you experienced that you have been blaming on your parents?

_____

_____

_____

_____

Do you think you need to forgive your parents for the choices that you have made? _____

After reading Ezekiel 18:19-32, how do you feel? _____

_____

_____

_____

_____

_____

What should you do now that you know you should take responsibility for your own actions and reaping? _____

_____

_____

A Word of Thought

We at time get stuck on generational curses without realizing that once we accept Christ and we walk obediently in His law that whatever our parents and the generations before them have done, does not negatively affect our future because we have chosen to walk in righteousness.

Are You Brave Enough?: Know Who is in Your Camp

Scripture: Judges 7:1-22

A godly warrior with 32,000 men was called by the Lord to lead a battle, but he was told to trim his army to a size that would not allow them to think they brought the victory themselves. So the Lord told Gideon to have the timid and the afraid to leave the mountain. Over half the men, 22,000 left the mountain. After coming down to 10,000 in size, Gideon was told, "There are still too many men"

(Judges 7:4). After an interesting method of sorting the army was devised and put into place (how the men drunk water from the spring), there were 300 men through whom Gideon would defeat the Midianites.

We know from a later reference that there had been about 120,000 Midianite fighters during this time (Judges 8:11). These were huge odds against Gideon's army. Gideon had some sense of defeat in his spirit because, "That night the LORD said, "Get up! Go down into the Midianite camp, for I have given you victory over them! But if you are afraid to attack, go down to the camp with your servant Purah. Listen to what the Midianites are saying, and you will be greatly encouraged. Then you will be eager to attack. So Gideon took Purah and

went down to the edge of the enemy camp"
(Judges 7:9-11).

There will be a time when you are afraid to
fight, even when the Lord has spoken to you
that victory shall be yours. Even in your fear
and lack of faith, God will give you the
opportunity to scope out the enemy's camp
and hear their words in order to be
encouraged. Often times your enemy is more
afraid than you are.

Now, undeterred, Gideon divided his men into
three companies, each with trumpets and clay
pots. Gideon was so confident that God was
with him and that his military approach would
succeed that he told the men to, "Watch me,
follow my lead" (Judges 7:17). In a short time,
the men approached the Midianite camp, blew

their trumpets, crashed their jars and began shouting, "For the Lord and for Gideon" (Judges 7:18). Then "the 300 trumpets sounded, and the Lord caused the men throughout the camp to turn on each other with their swords" (Judges 7:22). Two prominent Midianite leaders were captured and decapitated, and the ordeal ends. God got the credit. A 120,000 man army was defeated by a 300 man army with trumpets, crashing jars, and shouting.

Sometimes you have too many people in your camp. The people who have made themselves available to fight with you are actually afraid and timid. Just because a person says that he or she is willing to fight with you doesn't mean that they are going to be there with you in the battle. Be cognizant of who is in your camp.

Self-Exploration

Who can you really say is willing to go into battle with you? _____

_____

_____

Who or what are you fighting for? _____

_____

_____

Are you willing to go into battle by yourself?

_____

Do you know the motive behind why people call you their friend? _____

_____

_____

_____

A Word of Thought

Who you expect to go into battle with you may be the very person who is too timid and afraid to fight on your behalf or with you. Be aware of who is in your camp and be knowledgeable of their gift and how they can help you become victorious. Remember, it is not about the quantity of your camp, but the quality.

www.ingramcontent.com/pod-product-compliance
Lightning Source LLC
Chambersburg PA
CBHW071840020426
42331CB00007B/1799